AKULE

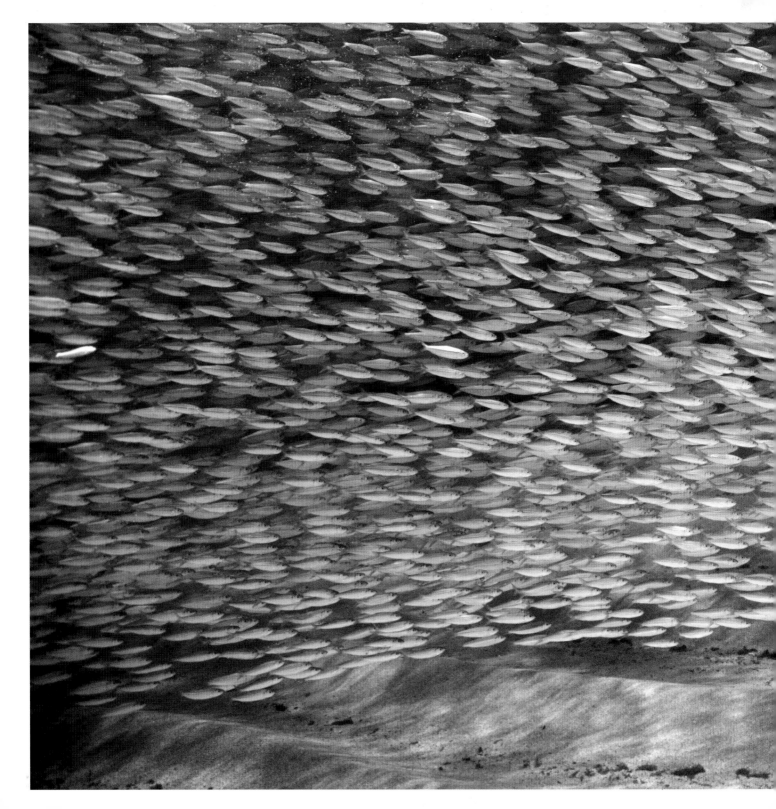

PHOTOGRAPHS BY WAYNE LEVIN

ESSAYS BY THOMAS FARBER AND FRANK STEWART

AKULE

AN EDITIONS LIMITED BOOK

*The Akule photography project was
funded in part through a Hawai'i State
Foundation on Culture and the Arts
Individual Artist Fellowship*

PUBLISHED BY
Editions Limited
P. O. Box 10150
Honolulu, Hawai'i 96816
editionslimited@hawaii.rr.com

ISBN 978-0-915013-55-5
LCCN 2010927177

Wayne Levin: www.waynelevinimages.com
Editions Limited: www.hawaiipublisher.com

Designed and produced by Barbara Pope Book Design
Printed in Singapore

FOR ELISE

Water lover and "street photographer" in the tradition of Cartier-Bresson and Brassaï, Wayne Levin took a Nikonos underwater camera into the surf in 1983. Phenomenally original, his brilliant, mysterious, black-and-white images of body surfers at Makapu'u on O'ahu in Hawai'i —were they flying? was that turbulence, water, or air?—had the force of revelation. Further below the surface, however, Levin was moving deeper into his art. Alone, free diving (with mask and fins) in Kealakekua Bay on the Big Island of Hawai'i, or in a kayak way, way offshore, he was in search of spinner dolphins and humpback whales. Which soon lured him further down, as if summoned, scuba diving to get eye-to-eye with, say, large pelagic hunters. One of his most compelling images is of an oceanic whitetip shark, very close, sole presence in the seeming void. Weighing the photograph, you grasp that in the vastness of that deep blue there are in fact two figures. One of them out of the frame, camera in hand. Talk about exposures!

By the early years of the new millennium, Levin had been in waters of Yap, Chuuk Lagoon, Bikini Atoll, and Cocos Island off Costa Rica. But back at home, in Kealakekua Bay, he'd found a new subject: schools of akule—bigeyed scad. 7 to 12 inches in length when adult, thousands of fish, tens of thousands, shoaling, swarming, flocking, herding, moving as if a single entity, densely-packed lives rotating, wheeling, spiraling. Shape-shifting congregations, morphing aggregations, phalanxes, clusters: located, observed, and captured—on film. So many, many evolutionary strategies! Wife, daughter, parents, siblings, and friends on shore, but in with the teeming akule, Levin was a party of one.

Resourceful—perennially a hungry if not starving artist—Levin would hike up a steep trail on the cliff over the bay, polarized sunglasses allowing him to discern fish schools through the surface. Back down on the beach, he'd then swim a course he hoped would converge with the akule. With only about 75 feet of visibility underwater, he had little margin for error. Free diving after a sequence of fast and slow breaths to oxygenate his lungs, he'd be down 25 to 50 feet, a minute or more at a time—never completely free of the downside risk of shallow water blackouts. What transpired was a dance, dialogue, or courtship of and with the akule. Levin's approach, their synchronized distractions, evasions . . . acceptance. Sometimes, for instance, he faced away from them, then slowly turned, and instead of moving away, the school would . . . come toward him. Or, as he advanced, the school would open, forming a tunnel for him. Entering, he'd be engulfed in thousands of fish.

THOMAS FARBER

Body surfers
Makapu'u, O'ahu 1983

So went a three-year obsession, until the akule seemed to disappear from the bay. The ineffable, once more disappearing into the murk? Or the ineffable, disappeared by (human) predators. Fished out? Over-fished? All of Levin's water art has been informed by his keen awareness of the plight of the ocean and the marvelous creatures it contains.

Of which, it might be said, Wayne Levin is one. Whales, they say, evolved from mammals that evolved from fish that came ashore. Unlike us, however, the whales were terrestrial creatures, but resumed full-time marine life. With Wayne—family man, opera lover, gourmet diner when he can afford it—you might say his default setting is water. Or that he responds powerfully to his inner fish. Attentive, persistent, remarkably determined without ever saying so, in the ocean he has found both his métier and (other) natural element.

The Sailor Who Fell From Grace with the Sea—title in English of a Yukio Mishima novel. Having spent much water time with Wayne Levin—having lost sight of him kayaking into the setting sun in pursuit of a whale, seen him vanish into the gloaming obscured by the flapping of a manta ray's wings—I believe Wayne has gone very, very deep, but has never, ever fallen from grace with the sea. Which, I would say, defines both his character and his art.

I first saw Wayne Levin's photographs of whales, spinner dolphins, and akule in 1989. Images crisscrossed by underwater light in Kealakekua Bay, they remain a wonder to me. Why are this artist's photographs so singular? Why do they evoke in me—in us—this paradoxical response: on the surface we see them as utterly factual, even documentary, and yet in their very insistence on clarity, they are saturated with reverence and inward deliberation.

In his most arresting images, Levin focuses his subjects so sharply that the normal obstacles to seeing them—the distortions created by seawater between the camera lens and the subjects, the distortions in the camera lens itself—seem to be absent. Their clarity creates the illusion that we are seeing underwater life through air rather than water. And yet we are certain of having entered an ocean world, with its spectrum of gray tones in the cloudy peripheries and backgrounds, and dramatic juxtapositions of bright opalescence and silky black. Individual fish and entire schools come toward us, streaked by rays of oceanic light and shadows, like strangers who have emerged from a dark night into the glare of a street lamp. These strangers hover cautiously, almost within the range of touch, then turn away to reenter the grainy depths.

FOR CENTURIES, akule have been bountiful here in Hawai'i. In earlier times, villages posted lookouts, kilo i'a, above the bays, to alert everyone to the akule's seasonal arrivals. Easy to see when gathering in the shallows, the dense schools would form riverine patterns, like ribbons blown aloft, unfurling scrolls, the tails of kites, silk scarves carried away in the wind, bursts of fireworks—then suddenly contract into a writhing sculpture, a vortex, unscrolling again and moving on.

The Hawaiian language distinguishes each growth stage of the species. The small ones, pāʻāʻā, are two to three inches long; halalū are five to six inches; and the adult akule are seven to twelve inches. The immature akule arrive in autumn. Too small for netting, the little halalū are caught by hook—sometimes without bait—bunching together tightly to feed. In spring, the schools return as mature fish. While observing the many kapu involved with fishing, entire communities of Native Hawaiians once swam out with baskets, or loaded their canoes with olonā nets to gather them. Today, commercial fishermen use aircraft and sonar to locate akule, then net them by the ton.

You never enjoy the world aright,
till the sea itself floweth in your veins . . .
Thomas Traherne

WAYNE LEVIN'S images command our attention whether or not we have any special knowledge about akule. What's harder to account for and name are the emotions and sensations they evoke in us.

The word *enthrallment* comes to mind, from Middle English and Old Norse: *en* (to put in) *thrall* (bondage, slavery). By extension, "to be bound as with a spell." But why do these particular underwater images enslave us, arrest our hearts, and stop our tongues? Why the involuntary inhalation at the sight of patterns made by schooling fish, as though we were encountering visual traces of grace? Soon enough, we tire of looking and we begin explaining. But in the first moments (or years) of reflection, we are mute.

MARTIN BUBER, in *The Rung of Love*, offers us this Hasidic saying:

> Question: It is written in Proverbs, *As face reflects face in water, so the heart of man reflects man.* Why does the verse read "in water" and not "in a mirror?" Answer: Man can see his reflection in water only when he bends close to it, and the heart of man, too, must lean down to the heart of his fellow; then one heart will see itself within the heart of the other.

So it is with us as we bend closer to the page or framed print, expecting something familiar, of great importance, to gaze back. Something about ourselves? About all of nature? About beauty?

IN 1986, scientist Craig Reynolds programmed the first elegant computer simulation of flocking birds. He reduced the complexity of the behavior—with its similarity to herding, schooling, and swarming—to three relatively simple directives:

1. Maintain a minimum constant distance from other individuals
2. Match velocities with closest neighbors
3. Move toward the perceived center of the group

Reynolds programmed these directives into a number of virtual on-screen birds, or as he termed them, "boids," and produced amazing results. "So realistic is the flocking of Reynolds's simple algorithms," writes Kevin Kelly in his book *Out of Control: The New Biology of Machines, Social Systems, and the Economic World,* "that biologists have gone back to their hi-speed films and concluded that the flocking behavior of real birds and fish must emerge from a similar set of simple rules. A flock was once thought to be a decisive sign of life, some noble formation only life could achieve."

But have Reynolds's reductive calculations truly revealed the nobility and complexity of something so extraordinary? The heart of man leans toward the heart of his fellow, and sees himself there. It's not likely that what is revealed can be computer generated. We would be mistaken to believe that, like Morpheus, we have peered into the true Matrix, our currently fashionable metaphor to explain the mystery of life.

PHYSICIAN and science writer Lewis Thomas describes having been "transfixed" by an encounter with underwater animal life as he gazed into a glass enclosure at the Tucson Zoo. Observing the swimmers eye to eye, he writes, "there was only one sensation in my head: pure elation mixed with amazement at such perfection." All at once, Thomas continues, one hemisphere of his scientifically trained mind began recalling facts about "the physiology of their breathing, the coordination of their muscles, their vision, their endocrine systems, their digestive tracts." Meanwhile, the other hemisphere "wanted no part of the science," or ever again to think of the graceful creatures before him as merely "collections of cells."

Thomas's scientific habits of mind finally won out. But the experience impressed on him the paradox of human perception: on the one hand, we are willing to submit ourselves to feelings of wonder; on the other, we are just as eager to have objects of wonder submit to the dissecting table.

"It lasted, I regret to say, for only a few minutes," Thomas writes, "and then I was back in the late twentieth century, reductionist as ever." Nevertheless, he continues, he had experienced "something worth remembering," that in the instant of losing the sense of awe, of being overwhelmed, he became "flattened," merely a detached observer.

Thomas is not saying, I think, that we are capable of only seeing in one of two opposing ways. Or that scientists invariably lose their amazement at the living world. Or that facts displace innocence. Rather, he is reminding himself and us of the numbing effects of rigid habits, conclusions, and beliefs.

WATER is 800 times denser than air. In this habitat—always moving, altered by depth, temperature, wave action, currents, tides, and the eddies from other life forms—fish are hypersensitive. They have specialized ways to measure and interpret sensations underwater. For instance, sense organs along the sides of their bodies—called the lateral line system—may, in some species, detect electrical nerve impulses produced by the muscle movement of other fish, or even the electrical field of the planet, enabling them to navigate on long migrations. With these organs, individual fish can accurately monitor the distance between themselves and others. In sharks, the lateral-line system is a series of pores. Electroreceptors in the pores identify the magnetic fields of prey, and lead sharks to a kill. To offset the shark's detection system, some prey species travel in closely knit schools, relying on their numbers to overwhelm the shark's senses, to make it difficult for the predator to single out and attack individuals, to accurately calibrate distance, movement, and space.

HUMANS, too, lose acuity and become flattened when their senses are overwhelmed—as they constantly are. When we speak, for example, the structure of our inner ears and our auditory neurons inhibit our hearing in complex ways—an explanation for why it's difficult to talk and listen at the same time. Georg von Békésy, who spent the latter part of his career at the University of Hawai'i, received the Nobel Prize in 1961 for his research on "sensory inhibition," explaining how and why our brains filter out loud, repetitive, painful, or even pleasurable sensory data by redirecting or muting our attention. Under such conditions, what we once perceived as beautiful is drained of wonder as our perceptors become anesthetized.

The best example of involuntary mental and physical sensory inhibition is sleep. Somehow, Levin's photographs wake us up. They alert us again to wonder at magnificence. Enthralled, we give his images our utmost attention. We become adrenalized, in the way we are brought to attention by hearing afresh certain music or seeing anew a face we love. Simone Weil considered this attentive, profoundly reverent state synonymous with prayer.

WHEN THE RECOGNITION of life's intense beauty wells up in us, the feeling is accompanied by another emotion that deepens it further—gratitude for our human capacity to see and acknowledge its presence. In gratitude, we allow the subjective *I* to recede, and give up the fear of losing our boundaries. We feel welcomed, like a guest, into our humanity and into the world. Elaine Scarry in her book *On Beauty* suggests that gratitude in the presence of beauty comes with the sense that the world wants us. The word *welcome*, she reminds us, means that one comes with the well wishes and consent of the being or place whose doors are opened. Host and guest, she writes, "each welcomes the other," and each "comes in accordance with the other's will."

In Wayne Levin's photographs of akule, we wonder at thousands of individuals cooperating in synchronous elegance, without a leader, and without dissent. We concede the possibility that being a Self in the natural world might mean existing not as "stuff that abides," to borrow Norbert Wiener's phrase, "but patterns that perpetuate themselves." We cease to be the hero in our own story and, for a moment, sense the world as more capacious than our isolated subjectivity.

WHERE TO BEGIN and where to end? The photographs and the photographer. Myself the viewer, and over my shoulder the invisible multitude of viewers I sense schooling in my peripheral vision. And within, a double self: belonging and yet aware of a painful separation from a congruous reality. I know language is incommensurable with Wayne Levin's photographs. A photographer friend of mine, summing up his impression, called them "tender." An apt word. Tender and precise, and without sentimentality, revealing the sorts of things that happen in this immense world.

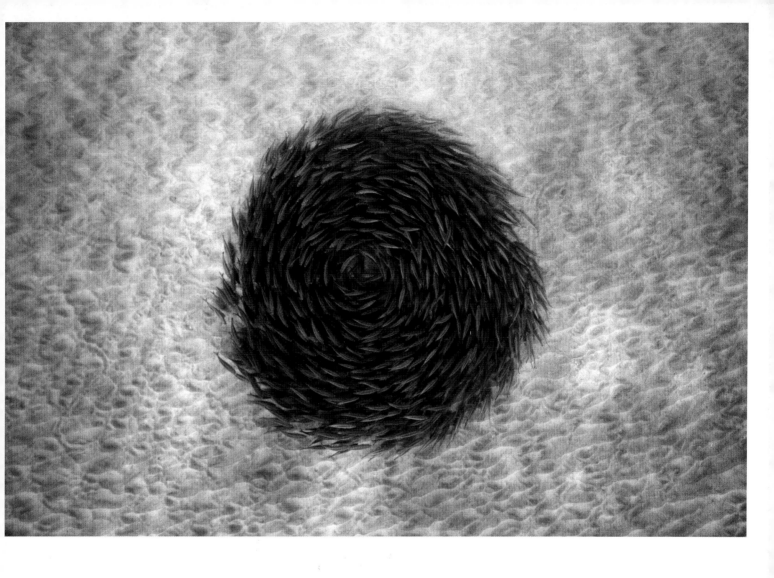

Akule pinwheel

Kealakekua Bay, Hawai‘i 2000

A small school circles counterclockwise, probably
feeding on tiny creatures stirred up from the bottom. **17**

School of akule surrounding
bluefin trevally ('ōmilu)
Kealakekua Bay, Hawai'i 2001
'Ōmilu are large, aggressive predators.
The adults tend to be solitary, but often
hunt in groups, as seen here.

Akule ball with eyestripe surgeonfish (palani)
Kealakekua Bay, Hawai'i 2000

19

Akule pyramid
Keauhou Bay, Hawaiʻi 2006

opposite
Akule tornado
Kealakekua Bay, Hawaiʻi 2000
*A portion of a much larger school swirls
to evade predators.*

Diver watching akule
Keauhou Bay, Hawaiʻi 2006
Diver Jon Hopcia positions himself between
a large school above and the reef below.

Bluefin trevally ('ōmilu) and amberjack (kāhala)
entering akule school
Kealakekua Bay, Hawai'i 2002
Sometimes, different species of predators
will work together.

opposite
Screen of akule
Kealakekua Bay, Hawai'i 2002
A line of akule along the edge of a coral reef.

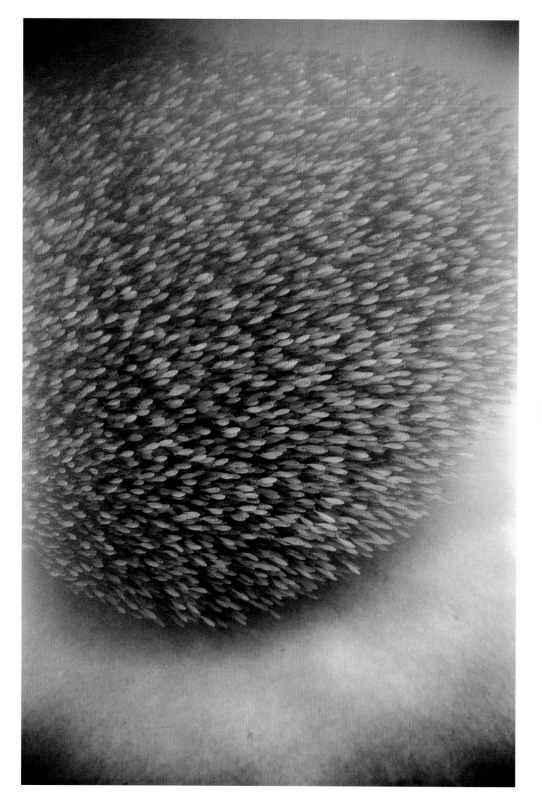

School of akule
Kealakekua Bay, Hawai'i 1999
*Though the school seems here to be
maintaining a constant shape, in the
next moment it bursts unpredictably.*

Filming akule
Keauhou Bay, Hawai'i 2006
Diver Glennon Gingo films a large school
looming over him in a dense but agile mass.

Flock of akule

Keauhou Bay, Hawai'i 2006

The presence of commercial fishermen using nets in
Keauhou Bay causes the school to skittishly dart from
place to place. Here, they gather over a deep drop-off,
before rapidly vanishing into the depths.

Elongated akule ball over sand
Waimea Bay, Oʻahu 2008
On a calm summer's day, the school gathers about
one hundred yards offshore in the bay famous for
its big waves in the winter months.

Column of akule

Kealakekua Bay, Hawai'i 2000

*In the upper right, the dim shapes of several ulua
can be seen. They are probably responsible for
the density of the school.*

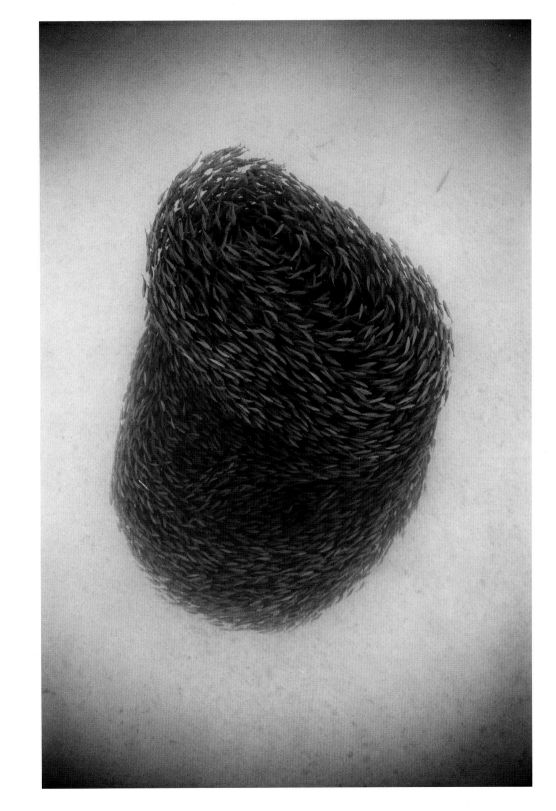

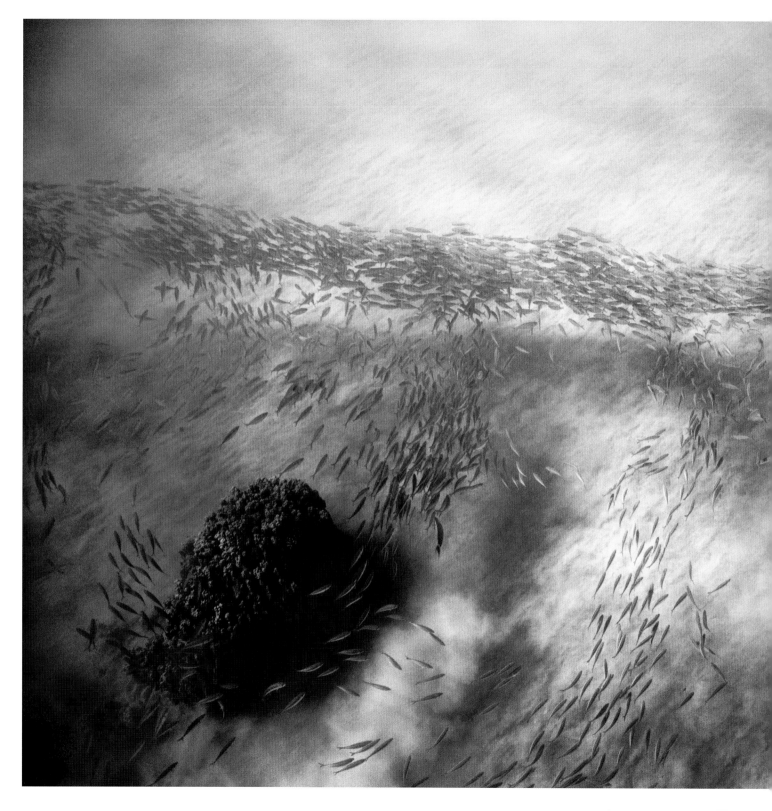

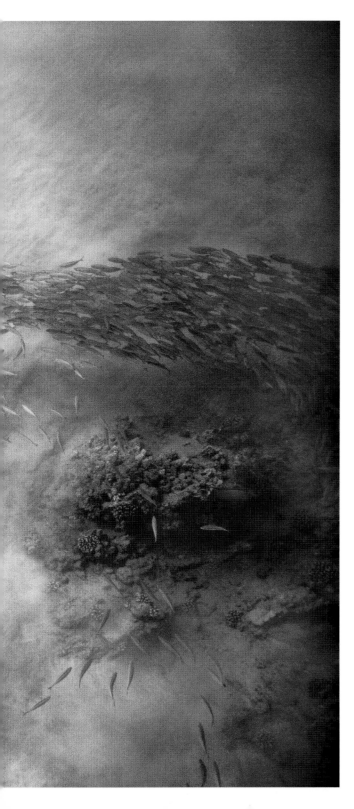

Akule strand

Kealakekua Bay, Hawai‘i 2002

Outlying smaller schools of akule form lines
as they join the larger school that's streaming
to a new location.

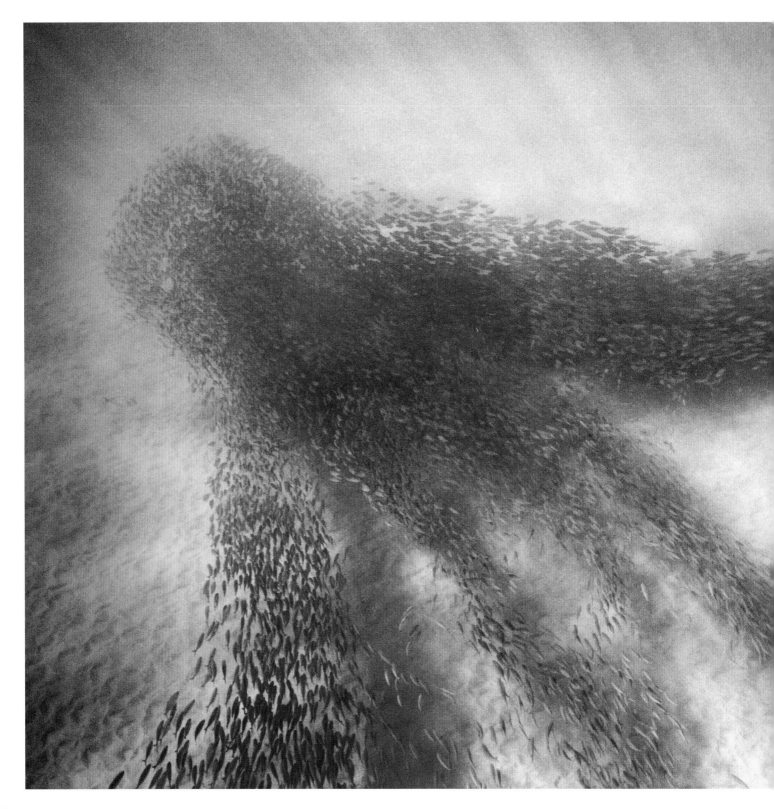

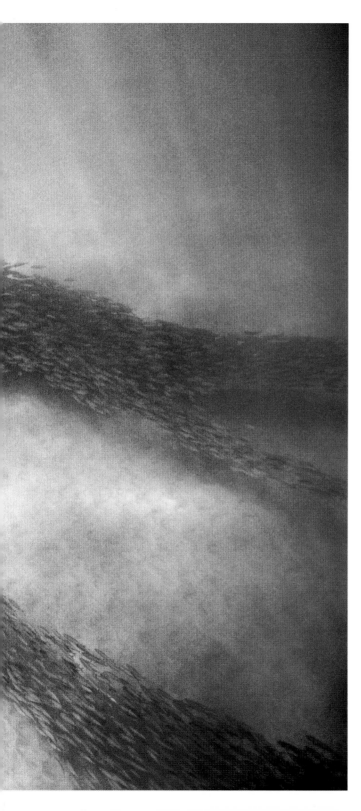

Fingers of akule
Kealakekua Bay, Hawaiʻi 2002
Funneling together from dispersed locations,
akule form a new school, eerily shaped like the
fingers of a hand sweeping along the ocean floor.

Bluefin trevally ('ōmilu) herding akule
Kealakekua Bay, Hawai'i 2000
'Ōmilu are shaping and herding
the school after chasing them three
or four hundred yards across the bay.

Line of akule #1
Kealakekua Bay, Hawai'i 2002
Akule merge to form a larger school
with 'ōpelu (mackerel scad) above.

opposite

Akule ring circling massive school
Kealakekua Bay, Hawai'i   2000
The edge of a massive school, to the right,
is encircled by a stream of akule, giving the
appearance of a planet with rings.

Ring of akule
Kealakekua Bay, Hawai'i   2001

High key akule
Keauhou Bay, Hawaiʻi 2006
The school hovers over a sandy channel that
leads to a drop-off. "High key" refers to the
white-on-white brightness of the image.

opposite
Wall of akule
Waimea Bay, Oʻahu 2008

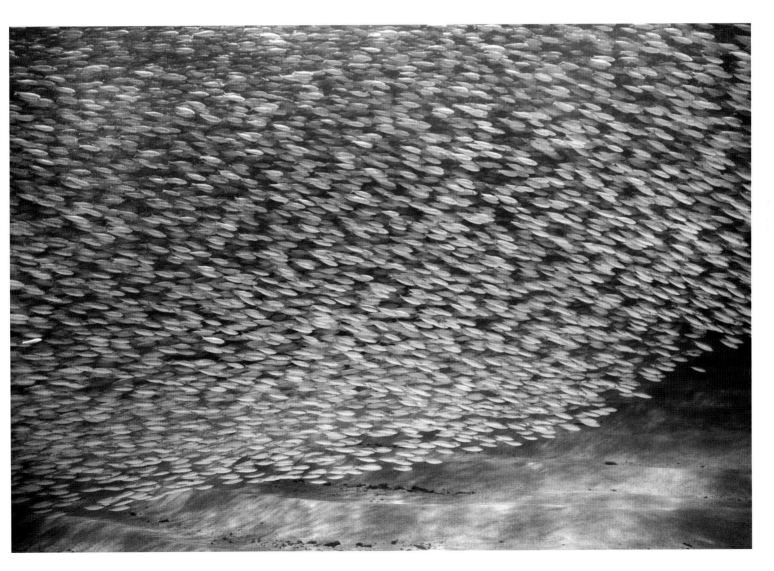

opposite
Within a school of akule
Keauhou Bay, Hawai'i 2006
A fish-eye view amid a school gliding over the reef.

Akule in sand channel
Keauhou Bay, Hawai'i 2006

Akule over sand formations
Waimea Bay, Oʻahu 2008

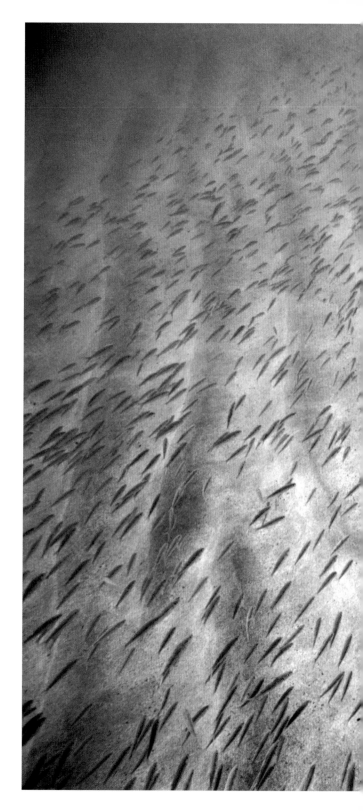

Akule beneath ocean surface
Waimea Bay, Oʻahu 2008
In shallow water very close to the surface, the school creates a reflection of broken light above it.

opposite
Line of akule #3
Waimea Bay, Oʻahu 2008

Akule and mooring
Keauhou Bay, Hawaiʻi 2003
A school gathers in murky water around
a mooring in the inner portion of the bay.

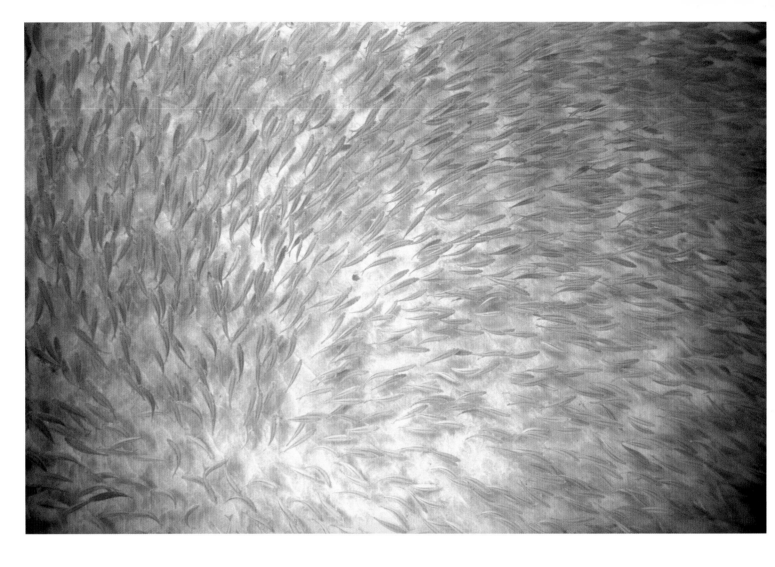

Swirling akule
Black Point, Oʻahu 2008
*In the early morning, a school of halalū
(juvenile akule) whirl off a rocky point
on the south shore of Oʻahu.*

Pattern of akule

Kealakekua Bay, Hawai‘i 2002

Circling akule
Kealakekua Bay, Hawaiʻi 2000

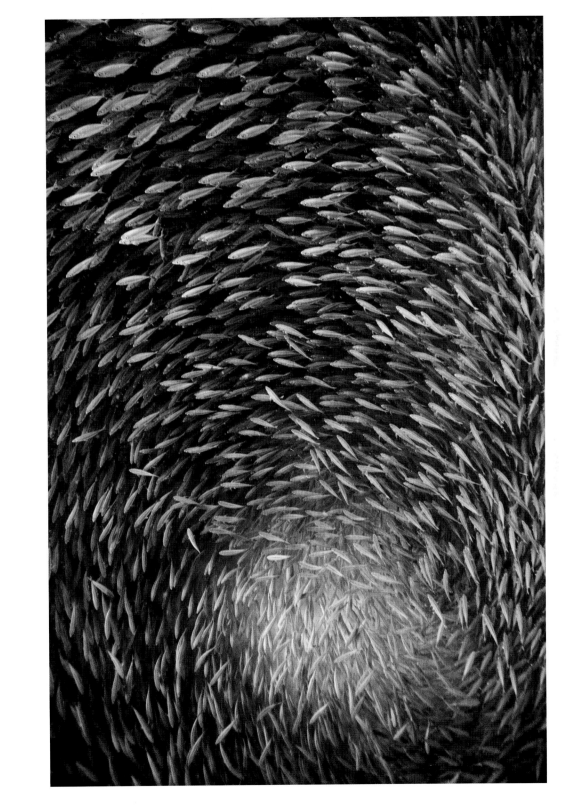

opposite
Huge school of rainbow runners (kamanu)
with akule
Kealakekua Bay, Hawai'i 2001

Akule loop
Keauhou Bay, Hawai'i 2006
Very aggressive kāhala (amberjacks) create a loop
in the school as the akule evade the hunters.

Amberjacks (kāhala) and akule over sand
Kealakekua Bay, Hawaiʻi   2002

opposite
Akule seascape
Keauhou Bay, Hawaiʻi 2006
A dispersed school glides over the reef
and sandy ocean floor.

Eyestripe surgeonfish (palani),
black triggerfish (humuhumu ʻeleʻele),
and bluefin trevally (ʻōmilu) with akule
Kealakekua Bay, Hawaiʻi 2002

Akule storm
Waimea Bay, Oʻahu 2008

Pufferfish (ʻoʻopu hue) with akule

Keauhou Bay, Hawaiʻi 2006

opposite

Akule tunnel with eight amberjacks (kāhala)
Keauhou Bay, Hawai'i 2006
A large group of kāhala carve out
a tunnel in the school.

Pattern of juvenile akule (halalū) and
rainbow runners (kamanu)
Kealakekua Bay, Hawai'i 2001
Very aggressive kamanu tear apart
a school of halalū.

Amberjacks (kāhala) and akule
Kealakekua Bay, Hawai'i 2000
The school becomes a wall as it evades
the large predators.

Bluefin trevally ('ōmilu) herding akule
Kealakekua Bay, Hawai'i 2000
Hunting together, the predators open
a gaping hole in the school.

Eagle ray (hīhīmanu) passing akule school
Keauhou Bay, Hawaiʻi 2006
A passing hīhīmanu has no interaction
with the school.

Amberjacks (kāhala) under a school of akule
Keauhou Bay, Hawai'i 2007
*The predators cautiously work a huge school
from underneath, rarely scattering them until
they are ready to take one akule at a time.*

Great barracuda (kākū) in a school of akule
Kealakekua Bay, Hawai'i 2001

Rainbow runners (kamanu) within a school of akule
Kealakekua Bay, Hawai'i 2001

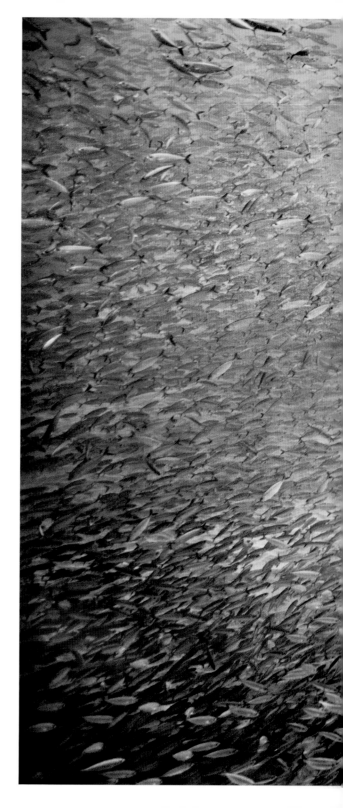

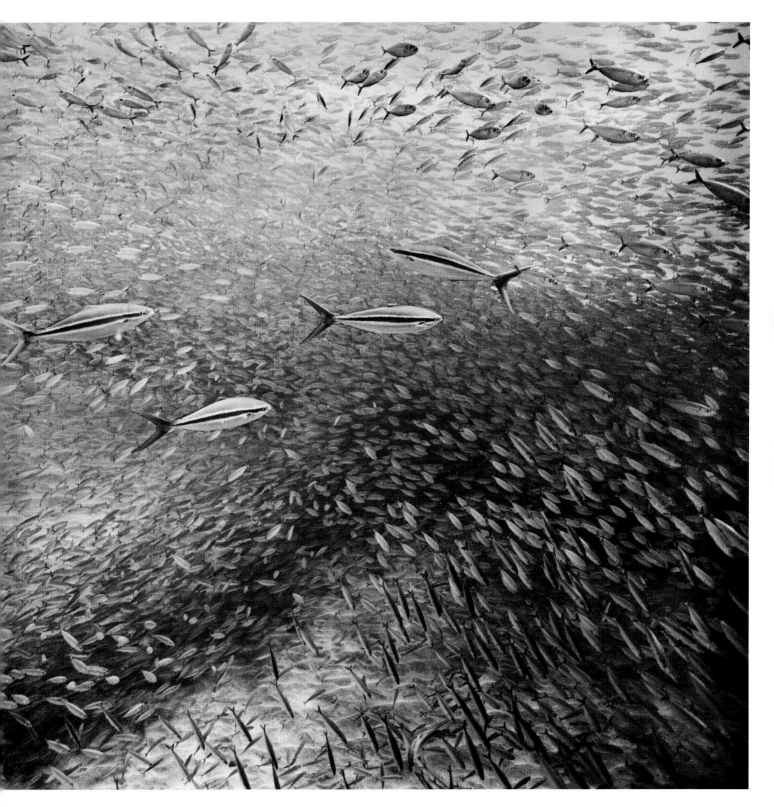

Rainbow runners (kamanu) hunting akule
Kealakekua Bay, Hawai'i 2001
Several large predators create havoc among the akule.

Great barracuda (kākū) stalking akule
Kealakekua Bay, Hawai'i 2002

Eagle ray (hīhīmanu) over a school of akule
Keauhou Bay, Hawai'i 2006

opposite
Two amberjacks (kāhala) under akule
Keauhou Bay, Hawai'i 2006

Amberjacks (kāhala) and bluefin trevally ('ōmilu) framed by akule

Kealakekua Bay, Hawai'i 2002

The school is scattered by the presence of hunters.

Amberjack (kāhala) and akule over coral reef
Keauhou Bay, Hawai'i 2007
*The watchful school seems to hover around
the large predator.*

Akule and sun rays
Keauhou Bay, Hawai'i 2008
Looking upwards toward the sun
as a school glides overhead.

Great barracuda (kākū) surrounded by akule
Kealakekua Bay, Hawai'i 2002
The school opens up for a barracuda.

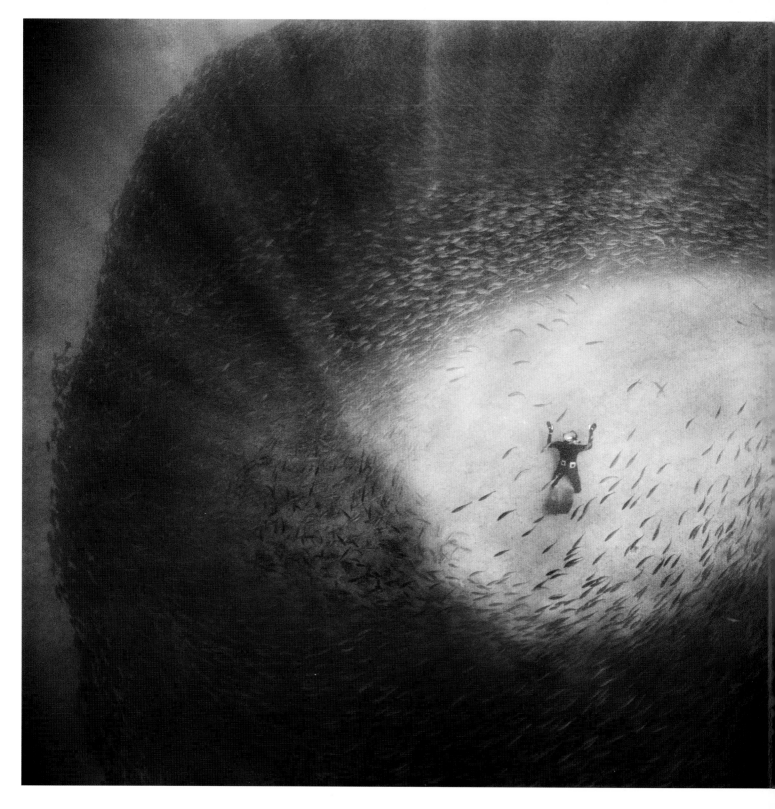

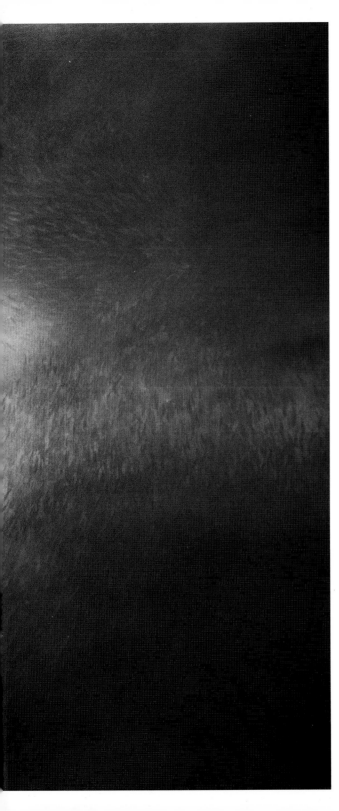

Freediver surrounded by akule
Kealakekua Bay, Hawai'i 2002
Canadian freediver Rick Waines kneels on the sand
in amazement as a large school encircles him.

Thomas Farber is author of *On Water* and *The
Face of the Deep* as well as works of fiction and the
epigrammatic. Recipient of Guggenheim, National
Endowment for the Arts, Rockefeller, and Fulbright
fellowships, Thomas Farber is Senior Lecturer in
English at the University of California, Berkeley
(visit www.thomasfarber.org).

Frank Stewart is a writer and editor who has taught
English at the University of Hawai'i at Mānoa since
1974. For the last twenty years, he has edited *Mānoa:
A Pacific Journal of International Writing*, published
by the University of Hawai'i Press. He is a recipient
of the Hawai'i Governor's Award for Literature.

Wayne Levin
www.waynelevinimages.com

Editions Limited
www.hawaiipublisher.com